BATMAN

THE BAT AND THE BEAST

BATMAN

THE BAT AND THE BEAST

Peter Milligan
Writer

Andy Clarke
Artist

David Baron
Colorist

Sal Cipriano
Letterer

Jock
Cover Artist

Batman created by Bob Kane

Mike Marts Editor-original series
Janelle Siegel Assistant Editor-original series
Bob Harras Group Editor-Collected Editions
Peter Hamboussi Editor
Robbin Brosterman Design Director-Books

DC COMICS
Diane Nelson President
Dan DiDio and **Jim Lee** Co-Publishers
Geoff Johns Chief Creative Officer
Patrick Caldon EVP-Finance and Administration
John Rood EVP-Sales, Marketing and Business Development
Amy Genkins SVP-Business and Legal Affairs
Steve Rotterdam SVP-Sales and Marketing
John Cunningham VP-Marketing
Terri Cunningham VP-Managing Editor
Alison Gill VP-Manufacturing
David Hyde VP-Publicity
Sue Pohja VP-Book Trade Sales
Alysse Soll VP-Advertising and Custom Publishing
Bob Wayne VP-Sales
Mark Chiarello Art Director

THE BAT AND THE BEAST
PART ONE

<TRY TO BE NICER TO HIM, CAN'T YOU? HE'S ONLY A CHILD.>

<ONE CANNOT AFFORD TO BE A CHILD IN TODAY'S RUSSIA.>

<GIVE HIM ANOTHER SHOT.>

<AND WHILE YOU'RE AT IT, GIVE HIM A *SHAVE*. HE'S GETTING MORE EYEBROWS THAN *BREZHNEV*.>

<POOR KID.>

TWELVE YEARS LATER...

<"BEAUTIFUL!">

<"EXQUISITELY, *UNBEARABLY* BEAUTIFUL.">

<MADE BY *PETER CARL FABERGÉ* IN 1901 FOR TSAR NICHOLAS II. AND NOW THE LATEST *TSAR* GIVES IT TO *YOU*.>

<HAPPY SEVENTEENTH BIRTHDAY, FYDOR!>

<EXTRAVAGANT, YES...BUT I KNOW HOW YOU LOVE *FABERGÉ*.>

<AND YOU'VE BEEN SO GOOD LATELY WITH MY LITTLE

<THEY WERE CAUGHT BY SURPRISE. THEY HADN'T RECKONED ON SOMETHING SO... *BIG*. SO...BIG AND TERRIBLE....>

<*WE*, ON THE OTHER HAND, WILL BE READY FOR THE CREATURE.>

<THE *BEAR*. IT LOOKS LIKE A BEAR. BUT IT IS MUCH MORE... AWFUL THAN ANY BEAR. THEY SAY HE SUCKS THE FLESH OFF THE BONES OF HIS VICTIMS.>

<N-NEVERTHELESS WE SHALL FACE IT LIKE CHECHENS.>

<GEORGIANS!>

<LIKE AZERBAIJANIS.>

<RUSSIANS!>

<IT'S SETTLED THEN. WE TRY TO OVER-THROW THE *TSAR*.>

<AND MAY GOD HELP US.>

"THE TSAR?"

REAL NAME BORIS STAVROGIN. RUNS THE MOSCOW UNDERWORLD. ALL COMPETITION HAS RECENTLY BEEN CRUSHED.

NOW HE'S TURNING HIS EYES ON OUR SWEET HOME TOWN.

OUR LOCAL MOBS WOULD HAVE SOMETHING TO SAY ABOUT THAT, SURELY.

THEY'RE STRIKING A DEAL, COMMISSIONER.

THERE'S GLOBALIZATION FOR YOU, I GUESS.

THE TSAR HAS GOT HOLD OF AN EX-SOVIET THERMO-NUCLEAR BOMB.

WITH THE HELP OF OUR LOCAL MOBSTERS HE PLANS TO SMUGGLE IT INTO GOTHAM AND HOLD THE CITY RANSOM.

WHAT DOES OUR MOB GET OUT OF IT?

WHERE WE GOIN', BOYS?

DUNNO. WE GOTTA FOLLOW THE RUSSKI'S BOY.

DAMN, I GOT GAS.

HEY, JOEY, STOP DA CAR A MINUTE, WILL YA?

YOU HEARD HIM, JOEY. STOP THE CAR.

OUR GOOD FRIEND THE DISGUSTING FAT PIG HAS GOT GAS.

I SEE YOU, MORRINO.

KKAKA KAAKK KAKA

UGNN!

DON'T HIT ME, BATMAN. THIS IS *SAM MORRINO!*

FAT MAN, YOU LOUSY SNITCH!

I'M A GOTHAMITE, JOEY--WHY SHOULD I HELP SOME *RUSSIAN* BLOW UP MY CITY?

UGHH HGHH HGG

<I'M SORRY TO CALL YOU LIKE THIS, SIR, BUT THERE'S TROUBLE...>

<MY DEAR MYSKIN, DO CALM DOWN. I'M SURE IT'S NOTHING WE CAN'T MANAGE.>

<WE'VE BEEN ATTACKED BY THE BATMAN!>

<INTERESTING.>

<NEVER REALLY BELIEVED IN HIM, I TH-THOUGHT HE WAS JUST SOME AMERICAN MYTH, LIKE JOHN WAYNE AND-->

--!

WHO IS THIS?

"THE RUSSIAN REFUSES TO TALK. HE'S TOO SCARED."

"OR TOO *LOYAL.*"

THAT'S NOT LOYALTY. THE TSAR *SCARES* HIM.

HEY, HE *SCARES* THE HECK OUT OF *ME.*

BUT MAYBE I'M GETTING TO THE AGE WHERE A LOT OF THINGS DO THAT.

MOSCOW...

I've come looking for a bomb. And I've found a foreign city.

Fewer fire escapes, for a start. Buildings spaced further apart.

Moving around becomes an interesting challenge.

It's almost a relief to find that criminals operate here...

...just like they do in Gotham.

THE BAT AND THE BEAST

<YOU HEARD HIM. LEAVE US IN PEACE.>

<I'LL ASK YOU ONE MORE TIME. I'M LOOKING FOR THE TSAR.>

<THE TSAR?>

<P-PLEASE.>

<PLEASE, DO NOT ASK HIM ABOUT THE TSAR!>

<IF YOU THINK I'D TELL YOU ANYTHING ABOUT THE TSAR, YOU MUST BE EVEN MORE STUPID THAN YOU LOOK.>

<AND BELIEVE ME, YOU DO LOOK PRETTY STUPID.>

<P-PLEASE... LEAVE US BE. WE ARE SIMPLY CONDUCTING A BUSINESS TRANSACTION.>

<I DON'T CARE HOW AFRAID YOU ARE. YOU'RE GOING TO TELL ME WHERE I CAN FIND THE TSAR.>

<YOU DON'T GET IT. MAYBE YOU'RE SOMETHING WHERE YOU COME FROM, BUT HERE...>

<...YOU'RE NOTHING.>

<TRUST ME.>

<I HAVE MANY WAYS TO MAKE YOU TALK TO ME.>

Maybe I thought this city wouldn't be so different from Gotham.

Maybe I thought I could follow the same script.

I was wrong.

HHHN!

<STOP!>

<TAKE OFF YOUR MASK AND STOP!>

"<LOOK AT HIM. HE'S NOT QUITE HUMAN.>"

"<HE'S A FREAK. AN ATHLETE. *MORE* THAN HUMAN.>"

"<AT LONG LAST...>"

"<...A LITTLE *COMPETITION.*>"

<IN THE NAME OF GOD, DIDN'T ONE OF YOU CRETINS *HIT* HIM?>

I keep seeing that man's face.

His eyes as he pulled the trigger.

As he blew himself into oblivion.

Even the Joker, with his manifold psychoses, has he ever done anything so shockingly insane?

But that's it. The guy didn't seem insane. He seemed calm.

As though he knew what he was doing.

As though there were no alternative.

SO FAR I'VE FELT LIKE A TOURIST.

THE CITY'S STILL STRANGE TO ME. I'VE GOT TO GET UNDER ITS SKIN.

SPEAKING OF WHICH, HOW'S THE DISGUISE?

ITCHY. IT'S LIKE WEARING A DEAD RACOON.

STICK WITH IT. WE NEED YOU UNDER-COVER IN MOSCOW, AND I'M ASSUMING YOU DON'T WANT THEM TO KNOW YOUR TRUE IDENTITY.

ANYTHING FROM OUR PRISONER?

HE'S EITHER LOYAL, STUPID, OR VERY, VERY AFRAID.

MY MONEY'S ON AFRAID. SOMEONE BLEW HIS BRAINS OUT TODAY RATHER THAN TALK ABOUT THE TSAR. THEY'RE ALL AFRAID OF HIM, JIM.

NO, *MORE* THAN AFRAID. THIS GOES DEEPER. THE TSAR HAS SOME-THING OVER THEM THAT WE'RE NOT SEEING.

WHATEVER IT IS...

...I'M GOING TO HAVE TO MAKE THEM EVEN MORE AFRAID OF ME.

DING-DONG DING

<--AND IF HE OFFERS YOU A DRINK, TURN IT DOWN. THEY THINK WE'RE ALL ALCOHOLICS ANYWAY.>

<Y-YES, COLONEL-GENERAL LUKZOV.>

<SO LET ME *CRUSH* HIM.>

<FIRST WE MUST KNOW OUR ENEMY BETTER. HOW AND WHY DID GOTHAM GIVE BIRTH TO THIS STRANGE CREATURE?>

<CONSIDER...>

<...IS HE UNIQUE TO GOTHAM--OR DO ALL MODERN AMERICAN METROPOLISES CREATE THESE SEMI-HUMAN MONSTERS?>

<YOUR FOOD WILL BE BROUGHT TO YOU.>

<BUT THE BAT?>

<IF I UNDERSTAND HIM CORRECTLY, HE WILL DO WHAT WE DID...>

"<...WHEN WE WANTED THE ATTENTION OF MOSCOW'S SHADOW WORLD.>"

<IT LOOKS LIKE A BAT... BUT IT IS MORE AWFUL THAN ANY BAT.>

<WHY DOESN'T HE DO SOMETHING ABOUT HIM? IT'S *HIS* CITY. THE TSAR SHOULD DEFEND IT!>

I understand.

<LISTEN...>

GN--GG!

<FORGET WHAT THE TSAR TOLD YOU. YOU CAN'T TRUST HIM.>

<THE TSAR HAS ALWAYS CARED FOR ME...>

<HE THREATENED TO DETONATE A NUCLEAR BOMB IN MOSCOW. THAT'S HOW MUCH HE CARES FOR YOU.>

<FABERGÉ!>

GNN!

THE TSAR BRINGS ME FABERGÉ!>

I understand how the Tsar controls the city.

<AH! MY SOLDIERS ALWAYS SCARE THE BEAR AWAY...>

<BUT YOU, YOU'RE MADE OF *STERNER STUFF.*>

<NOT QUITE HUMAN. MORE THAN HUMAN. BUT QUITE BEAUTIFUL...>

<WHO ARE YOU?>

<I READ ABOUT YOU IN AN INTERNATIONAL HERALD TRIBUNE THAT GOT WASHED DOWN HERE. YOU'RE BIG NOISE IN GOTHAM CITY.>

<BUT YOU'VE PROBABLY ALREADY NOTICED.>

<THIS ISN'T GOTHAM CITY.>

Even the tunnels beneath Moscow have their surprises.

<YOU'RE STAYING HERE WITH ME.>

<WHICH WAY DID THE BEAR GO? DID YOU SEE?>

<MY NAME'S PETR. WOULD YOU LIKE TEA?>

<YOU'RE AMERICAN, YOU MIGHT PREFER COFFEE.>

<THESE TUNNELS. WHERE DO THEY LEAD?>

<STAY PUT... OR I'LL HAVE NO OPTION BUT TO SET MY BOYS ONTO YOU.>

<YOUR BOYS?>

Not that I'm surprised by anything anymore.

<YOU MEAN THIS CLUMSY VOLUMETRIC DISPLAY?>

THE BAT AND THE BEAST
PART THREE

<AT LEAST STAY A WHILE AND TALK. TELL ME, HOW *ARE* THINGS IN GOOD OLD AMERICA?>

<ARE THE DUKES OF HAZARD STILL THE NATION'S FAVORITES?>

<THAT DAISY DUKE SURE IS PRETTY.>

<YOU DON'T GET OUT MUCH, DO YOU?>

<YOU BETTER BELIEVE IT, MAN. AND IT GETS LONELY STUCK DOWN HERE.>

<SO COME UP TO THE SURFACE.>

<ARE YOU CRAZY? IT'S *SCARY* UP THERE.>

<IT'S *CHAOS.*>

<BELIEVE ME, BAT TOVARISCH. YOU'RE BETTER OFF DOWN HERE. MOSCOW...IT ISN'T SAFE.>

<MOSCOW IS A JUNGLE!>

<...BUT THAT DOESN'T MEAN HE SHOULD BE TAKEN LIGHTLY. HE'S BEATEN SOME SERIOUS PLAYERS. PEOPLE LIKE *THE JOKER*.>

<I DON'T SUPPOSE YOU'VE HEARD OF *THE JOKER*?>

<N-NO, MASTER. HE SOUNDS... *AMUSING*.>

<HE ISN'T *AMUSING*. HE'S PROBABLY THE SINGLE MOST PSYCHOTIC KILLER AMERICA HAS PRODUCED.>

<AND THAT, MY FRIEND, IS *SAYING* SOME-THING.>

<LET ME ATTACK THE BAT AGAIN. THIS TIME...>

<YOU'RE NOT *LISTENING!*>

<THE JOKER IS A GRINNING KILLING MACHINE! WITHOUT APPARENT *WEAKNESS!*>

AWOWWW!

<AND YET THE BATMAN HAS DEFEATED HIM. TIME AND TIME AGAIN.>

<BUT *YOU* THINK YOU CAN JUST WALTZ UP TO BATMAN AND GET THE BETTER OF HIM ANY TIME YOU *WANT?*>

<*PLEASE*, MASTER.>

<I DON'T WANT TO BE WHIPPED ANY-MORE.>

<LISTEN TO ME, AND I WON'T *HAVE* TO WHIP YOU.>

<IT WILL TAKE *PLANNING* TO DEFEAT BATMAN.>

<WE MIGHT HAVE TO GIVE YOU SOME OF THAT *MEDICINE* THAT MAKES YOU FEEL SO SPECIAL.>

<PLEASE...>

<...DON'T WANT TO TAKE MEDICINE ANYMORE. I FEEL SICK AFTER. IT'S *POISON*.>

<DO YOU REALLY THINK I'D GIVE YOU ANYTHING THAT WAS *BAD* FOR YOU?>

<HAVE I NOT CARED FOR YOU? AFTER THOSE BAD MEN KILLED YOUR FATHER...DID I NOT TREAT YOU LIKE MY *OWN SON*?>

<THE BAT... HE...HE *SAID* SOMETHING ABOUT YOU.>

<WHAT, FYODOR? TELL ME, WHAT DID HE SAY?>

<HE SAID... YOU'RE AN EVIL CRIMINAL MANIAC.>

\<TSAR?\>

\<TS-TSAR...IT IS I, ROGACHENOK, KINGPIN OF BRYANSK OBLAST.\>

\<ROGACHENOK....\>

\<...WHAT'S THIS I HEAR ABOUT YOU HANGING OUT WITH THE BATMAN?\>

HE...HE'S HURTING US. EARNINGS ARE DOWN. THE KINGPINS...>

<THEY'RE... *SCARED.*>

<KINGPIN MEREB THE BLOODTHIRSTY HAS DEVELOPED A NERVOUS TIC. KRYUKOV THE WIDOW-MAKER...>

<...HE IS NOW TOO SCARED TO LEAVE HOME AT NIGHT.>

<I-IS THAT IT? IS...IS THAT THE *BOMB?*>

<NO, IT'S A RUSSIAN DOLL, YOU IDIOT.>

<WHAT THE HELL DO YOU *THINK* IT IS?>

KNNG KNNG KNNG

<I-ISN'T IT *DANGEROUS?*>

<B-BANGING IT LIKE THAT?>

<RELAX, ROGANCHENOK.>

<TELL THE OTHER KINGPINS TO RELAX, TOO.>

<CAN I TELL THEM THAT THE BEAR WILL KILL THE BAT?>

<SOON. RIGHT NOW THE BEAR IS GOING THROUGH A...A DIFFICULT STAGE. HOWEVER...>

<...THERE'S MORE THAN ONE PATHETIC CREATURE IN MOSCOW WHO'LL DANCE TO MY TUNE.>

Is it working?

Are they afraid of me yet?

Are they afraid enough?

<I *WARNED* YOU NOT TO STRAY FROM THE TOURIST ROUTE...>

<...THOUGH, OF COURSE, THAT WAS BEFORE I KNEW WHO YOU *WERE*.>

<COLONEL-GENERAL LUKZOV...>

<...GIVE ME TWO MORE DAYS AND I'LL BRING THE TSAR DOWN.>

<I'LL RID MOSCOW OF HIM FOR GOOD.>

<TAKE HIM, BOYS.>

<LUKZOV-- WE'RE ON THE *SAME* SIDE.>

I don't want to hurt them.

<HANDS IN THE AIR!>

<HOW DID YOU FIND ME?>

POLICY TO TAP THE PHONES OF ALL SUSPICIOUS VISITORS.>

HAVE A PARTICULARLY CLOSE RELATIONSHIP WITH COMMISSIONER GORDON OF GOTHAM CITY.>

<THE KINGPINS, THEY'RE GETTING *SCARED*.>

<I'M MAKING PROGRESS!>

GNNN!

<PROGRESS, YES. THAT'S WHAT I THOUGHT.>

<FIFTEEN YEARS AGO.>

I really don't want to hurt them.

KKSSHH

But I might *have* to...

If I don't hurt them first...

FUDDAFUDDAFUDDA

...they'll end up shooting each other.

<S-STOP OR I'LL-->

--!

<I'M AIMING AT YOUR *FACE*, BATMAN.>

<THE LAST TIME I SHOT A MAN IT GAVE ME NIGHTMARES.>

<DON'T MAKE ME HAVE ANY MORE NIGHTMARES.>

<...YOU LOOK LIKE *DEATH*.>

<HAVE YOU BEEN DRINKING AGAIN, NIKOLAI?>

<A FEW TOASTS.>

<YOU KNOW HOW VODKA OILS THE WHEELS OF THIS CITY.>

<AND WHAT ABOUT YOUR HIGH BLOOD PRESSURE? SVETI WORRIES ABOUT YOU, YOU KNOW.>

<I THOUGHT THE ONLY THING SHE WORRIED ABOUT WAS AMERICAN POP STARS AND ENGLISH HOMEWORK.>

<I MIGHT BE LATE. I'LL SLEEP IN THE SPARE ROOM.>

<NIKOLAI, YOU'D TELL ME IF SOMETHING WAS THE MATTER, WOULDN'T YOU?>

<SAY GOOD-NIGHT TO SVETI FOR ME.>

THE BAT AND THE BEAST
PART FOUR

<THEN I SAY, TSAR, THIS IS *ME* YOU'RE TALKING TO. ROGACHENOK OF BRYANSK OBLAST. I TELL HIM THE KINGPINS AIN'T HAPPY.>

<YEAH, RIGHT TO HIS FACE.>

<THIS *BAT* IS BAD FOR BUSINESS, I SAY. SO WHADDYA GONNA DO ABOUT IT? AND HE SAYS WE SHOULD ALL RELAX.>

<OH, AND I SAW THE BOMB. *HHMM?* IS IT *BIG?*>

<WELL, LET'S JUST SAY YOU DON'T WANT TO BE STANDING NEAR IT WHEN IT GOES-->

<HUH?>

<DON'T STOP BECAUSE OF ME.>

<HOLY-->

<AMERICAN PIG!>

BUDDA BUDDA BUDDA

UGHH!!

<YOU WERE TALKING ABOUT THE BOMB, ROGACHENOK.>

<I WANT TO HEAR ALL ABOUT THE BOMB.>

UGN—!

<H-HELP ME OUT HERE, GUYS! HE'S JUST A BIG LUMP IN A FREAKY COSTUME.>

<WHAT ARE YOU? SCARED?>

<SEE? THEY'RE STARTING TO GET THE MESSAGE.>

<NOW TELL ME ABOUT THAT BOMB.>

<I DIDN'T SEE ANY BOMB. I WAS LYING.>

<I LIE ALL THE TIME.>

<I DON'T BELIEVE YOU.>

<...NO SIGN OF ANY TROUBLE.>

<BUT OUR DAUGHTER IS REALLY BEING A PAIN. SHE THINKS YOU'RE OVER-REACTING.>

<TELL HER I'VE SENT SOME OF MY BEST MEN TO WATCH OVER YOU. THAT'S HOW WORRIED I AM.>

<I DON'T KNOW HOW LONG IT'LL BE FOR. AND I DON'T CARE IF SVETI DOESN'T LIKE IT.>

<HE SAID-->

<YEAH, I HEARD. TELL HIM-->

<OH MY GOD.>

<THE TSAR KILLED HIS FATHER?>

<WHAT I HEARD, THE FATHER TREATED THAT HAIRY KID WORSE THAN ANYONE.>

<I MEAN, OKAY, HE WAS A FREAK, BUT HE WAS STILL HIS SON, RIGHT?>

<THE BEAR'S DAD, HE STILL THOUGHT WE WERE BACK IN THE OLD DAYS.>

<WHEN THE SOVIET UNION TRIED TO WIN THE COLD WAR WITH OLYMPIC MEDALS.>

<IS THIS IT?>

<Y-YEAH.>

<IF YOU GET THROUGH HIS SECURITY IN ONE PIECE...P-PLEASE... PLEASE DON'T TELL HIM IT WAS ME WHO BROUGHT YOU HERE...>

<I-I GOT A WIFE AND TWO GIRLFRIENDS WHO DEPEND ON ME.>

"<YOU DON'T KNOW WHAT THE TSAR'S LIKE.>"

<GOOD WORK. ARE BOTH OF OUR GUESTS WELL?>

<UPSET? YES, I SHOULD IMAGINE THEY'RE VERY-->

<RASIF, GO SEE WHAT ALL THAT NOISE IS ABOUT.>

BUDDA BUDDA BUDDA

<CAN'T YOU GUYS GO ONE WEEK WITHOUT GETTING SMASHED OUT OF YOUR SKULLS?>

<DMITRI?>

<WHAT HAPPENED, DMITRI?>

--GHH!

I've come a long way for this.

I have worked hard to make the criminals of Moscow *fear* me.

I must not fail now.

<HAVEN'T YOU EVER WONDERED WHAT IT WOULD FEEL LIKE...>

<...TO BE THOROUGHLY OBLITERATED?>

<STAVROGIN!>

<LEAVE THE BOMB ALONE!>

<TO RETURN TO A STATE OF PURE, UNFORMED NON-BEING.>

<YOU HAVE TWENTY SECONDS... BEFORE YOU'LL FIND OUT HOW THAT FEELS.>

<THIS IS INSANE! IF THE BOMB GOES OFF WE'LL ALL DIE.>

<IT WOULD BE FASCINATING TO STAY AND TALK--->

<--BUT IT LOOKS LIKE YOU'RE GOING TO BE BUSY.>

Eighteen... Seventeen...

TICK TOCK TICK TOCK...

Sixteen... Fifteen...

TICK TOCK

<STAVROGIN! COME BACK HERE!>

<FOR GOD'S SAKE! TSAR!>

TICK

<MUSHROOM SOUP?>

<COME, PRETTY ONE, YOU SHOULD EAT. I LIKE A LITTLE MEAT ON MY BABUSHKAS.>

<SHE IS NOT YOUR BABUSHKA!>

<NOW GET YOUR FILTHY HANDS AWAY FROM HER!>

<SHE'S NOT HUNGRY. HOW COULD SHE BE HUNGRY?>

<MAMA...>

<YOUR MOTHER'S GOT A NASTY MOUTH. SHE SHOULD REMEMBER THAT THESE FILTHY HANDS COULD DO TERRIBLE THINGS TO YOU IF I WANTED THEM TO.>

UGHN!

<LEAVE HER ALONE! PLEASE! PLEASE DON'T HURT HER!>

<STOP IT.>

<YOU HEARD ME, GEORGY. STOP IT.>

<THIS IS NONE OF YOUR BUSINESS, FYODOR.>

<I DON'T WANT YOU TO TOUCH THEM.>

<I-IT'S OKAY, MAMA. THAT... CREATURE...>

<IT WON'T LET THEM... HURT US.>

<DON'T BE FOOLED, LITTLE GIRL.>

<IF THE TSAR TELLS HIM TO TEAR YOU TO SHREDS--THAT'S EXACTLY WHAT HE'LL DO.>

IT'S EMPTY, JIM.

A BIG, EMPTY METAL CASE. NO NUCLEAR WARHEAD. NO URANIUM. JUST A MECHANISM THAT WENT TICK-TOCK.

...BUT BY THE TIME I FOUND THAT OUT, THE TSAR WAS GONE.

SO MAYBE NOW YOU CAN COME HOME.

THE CITY ISN'T EXACTLY FALLING APART WITHOUT YOU...BUT WE COULD SURE USE YOUR *HELP* AROUND HERE...

STRAVROGIN PUT A LOT OF EFFORT INTO CONVINCING ME AND OTHERS THAT HE HAD A LIVE THERMO-NUCLEAR WEAPON.

I CAN'T LEAVE UNTIL I FIND OUT WHY...

<I WANT THE GOTHAM BAT'S SEVERED HEAD PICKLED IN VODKA...>

<...AND DELIVERED TO ME WITHIN A DAY, COLONEL-GENERAL LUKZOV.>

<OR--->

<OR YOUR PRECIOUS WIFE AND DAUGHTER WILL FIND AN ANSWER TO THAT HOARY OLD QUESTION...>

<...IS THERE A FATE WORSE THAN *DEATH?*>

<I'VE GOT A GOOD IDEA WHERE YOU'RE HOLDING THEM. I MIGHT SEND MY BOYS IN.>

<YOUR *BOYS?*>

<ARE THESE THE SAME BOYS WHO TRIED TO FREE THE *HOSTAGES* AT *BESLAN?*>

<HOW MANY DIED IN THAT SCHOOL, LUKZOV? *THREE HUNDRED,* WASN'T IT?>

<I WOULD ALSO LIKE THE BAT'S EARS MOUNTED ON A HOLY IKON.>

<WHY ARE YOU SO OBSESSED WITH DESTROYING BATMAN?>

<ONCE HE'S GONE...GOTHAM WILL BE WIDE OPEN.>

<WITHOUT THE BAT, I'M SURE THE GOTHAM POLICE ARE AS INEFFECTUAL AS THEIR *MOSCOW BRETHREN.*>

<YOU BELIEVED YOU COULD WRIGGLE OUT OF MY GRASP, COLONEL-GENERAL.>

<THAT WAS VERY STUPID.>

B-BATMAN?

<I TH-THINK I KNOW HOW WE CAN BRING DOWN THE TSAR. WE NEED TO MEET AND DISCUSS.>

<I'LL BE AT THE SOUTH SIDE OF THE SOLZHENITSYN STATUE, AT THE TOP OF THE AVENUE OF DISSIDENT WRITERS. M-MEET ME THERE AT MIDNIGHT...>

<SOUNDS AS THOUGH YOU'RE SHIVERING, COLONEL-GENERAL. ARE YOU OKAY?>

<TH-THIS AVENUE IS NOTORIOUS FOR ITS ICY WINDS.>

<SOME SUPERSTITIOUS OLD WOMEN BELIEVE THEY ARE THE HOWLING GHOSTS OF EXECUTED WRITERS.>

<MIDNIGHT, BATMAN.>

<PLEASE DON'T LET ME DOWN.>

"<IF THE TARGET APPROACHES FROM THE EAST...>"

<...POSITION TWO WILL SEE HIM FIRST. BUT I'LL STILL BE ABLE TO GET A SHOT OFF.>

<WE DON'T KNOW WHAT KIND OF TECHNOLOGY THE AMERICAN HAS AT HIS DISPOSAL...SO AS SOON AS YOU GET TO YOUR POSITIONS I WANT COMPLETE RADIO AND PHONE SILENCE.>

<THERE MUST BE NO POSSIBILITY OF THE TARGET ESCAPING.>

<WITH ALL THIS SHOOTING, THE SOLZHENITSYN STATUE IS LIKELY TO SUFFER EXTENSIVE DAMAGE, COLONEL-GENERAL SIR.>

<WE'LL DO WHAT WE USUALLY DO.>

<BLAME IT ON TERRORISTS.>

"<TIME, PAVLO?>"

<TWENTY SECONDS LATER THAN THE LAST TIME YOU ASKED, SIR. FIVE TO TWELVE.>

<I THINK MY EYES ARE GOING. I KEEP THINKING I SEE HIM. TH-THERE.>

<JUST SHADOWS, SIR. AND YOUR IMAGINATION.>

<THIS IS OUR CHANCE.>

<SIR?>

<WH-WHO KNOWS... THE BATMAN COULD BRING DOWN THE TSAR AND THE BEAR FOR GOOD. WE'D REALLY HAVE A CHANCE TO CLEAN UP THIS CITY.>

<AND WHAT ABOUT YOUR WIFE AND DAUGHTER?>

<THEY'RE YOUR *FAMILY*.>

<AND MOSCOW'S SUPPOSED TO BE MY CITY.>

<IS IT SO *BAD*, LIVING UNDER THE TSAR? HE KEEPS THE OTHER KINGPINS PRETTY MUCH UNDER CONTROL.>

<HE TREATS THE CITY LIKE HIS PERSONAL PLAYGROUND, THE POLICEMEN LIKE HIS SERFS.>

<TIME, PAVLO?>

<M-MIDNIGHT, SIR. THE STROKE OF MIDNIGHT.>

<DAMN IT! WHY AREN'T THOSE IDIOTS ANSWERING THEIR PHONES?>

<YOU TOLD THEM ALL TO MAINTAIN PHONE SILENCE, SIR.>

<I THINK... I THINK I SEE HIM, SIR...>

<NOW WE HAVE HIM.>

HGMMM!

<...QUITE OBVIOUS FROM YOUR VOICE THAT SOMETHING WAS WRONG. I TOOK A *PRECAUTION...*>

<...CHECKED OUT THE POSITIONS *I'D* TAKE IF I WAS TO SET A TRAP. YOU'LL FIND THE OTHER SNIPERS IN A SIMILAR CONDITION.>

<BUT WHAT MADE YOU CHANGE YOUR MIND, COLONEL-GENERAL? YOU PUT ALL THIS EFFORT INTO SETTING ME UP, THEN...>

<I-I REMEMBERED THE TSAR...HOW HE SPOKE TO ME THE LAST TIME WE MET. LIKE I WAS THE LOWEST FORM OF LIFE IMAGINABLE.>

<LIKE HE KNEW HE COULD MAKE ME DANCE LIKE THAT DAMNED *BEAR* OF HIS.>

<OH GOD! *THE BEAR!*>

<ANNA! SVETI!>

<STOP BLUBBERING, FYODOR. WE AGREED THERE'D BE NO MORE *PETULANCE.* I SIMPLY WON'T ALLOW IT, UNDERSTAND?!>

"<LUKZOV MUST BE TAUGHT A LESSON!>"

<WH-WHAT'S WRONG? WHY IS HE LOOKING AT US...LIKE THAT?>

<IT'S OKAY, MOM. THE BEAR IS OUR FRIEND. OUR GUARDIAN ANGEL. HE WOULDN'T HURT US.>

<YOU WOULDN'T...>

<...WOULD YOU?>

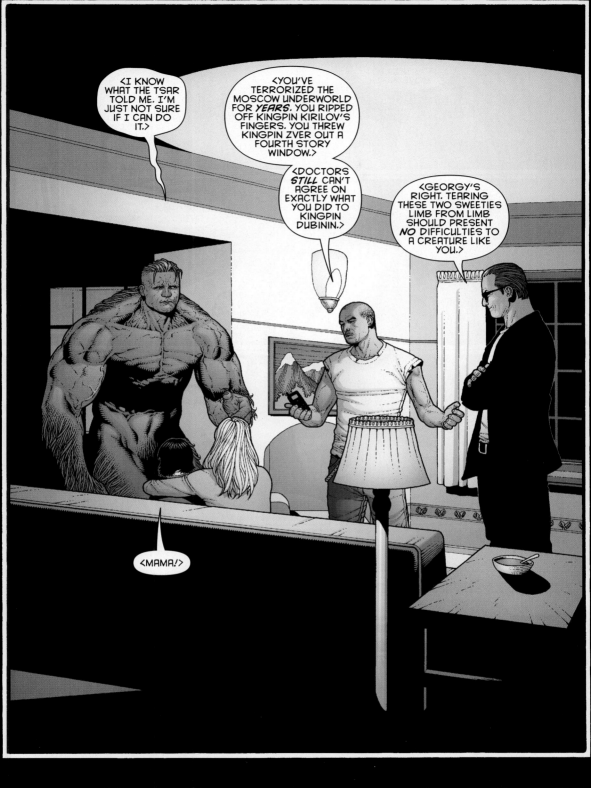

THE BAT AND THE BEAST
PART FIVE

<I DON'T BELIEVE THIS. THE TERRIBLE BEAR IS ACTUALLY *PROTECTING* THEM.>

<WHAT KIND OF A WILD ANIMAL *ARE* YOU?>

<FUNNY.>

<I WAS THINKING THE SAME THING ABOUT YOU.>

<TH-THANK YOU...NOW... NOW YOU CAN LET US GO.>

<THAT CAN'T HAPPEN.>

<IF YOU WALK OUT OF HERE ALIVE, THE TSAR WILL NAIL SEVERAL OF OUR DELICATE PARTS TO THE FLOOR.>

<IF ONLY YOU WERE FIVE HUNDRED POUNDS HEAVIER I WOULDN'T NEED A BEAR. YOU WOULDN'T DISOBEY ME, WOULD YOU, *PUSHKIN?*>

<HHMM? *YOU* WOULDN'T DISAPPOINT YOUR DADDY, WOULD YOU, MY SWEET?>

GGGR... RRR...RRR

Too late.

Don't let me be too late.

<BACK OFF! IF THE COLONEL-GENERAL'S DAUGHTER DIES, YOUR CAREERS GET WASHED DOWN THE MOSKVA.>

<HE'S GOT A POINT. I DON'T WANNA BE KNOWN AS ONE OF THE COPS WHO KILLED LUKZOV'S GIRL.>

<BACK OFF SLOWLY... GIVE HIM ROOM.>

AGHKK!

GGNN!

<THIS IS A MOSCOW POLICE MATTER. WE HAD IT UNDER CONTROL.>

<RIGHT, SO I NOTICED.>

<WHERE'S THE BEAR?>

<H-HE SAVED US. THEY WANTED HIM TO KILL US, BUT HE SAVED US.>

<NOW HE'S GONE.>

Blood. He must have taken a bullet.

He's hurt.

But how badly?

What does it take to stop a creature like that?

<...BELIEVE THOSE RUMORS AT YOUR PERIL, KINGPIN RAFIS. THE BEAR IS JUST AS FIERCE AND LOYAL AS EVER...>

<...AND YOU AND THE OTHER KINGPINS...>

<...YOU'D BETTER REMEMBER THAT.>

<HE WANTED TO SEE YOU, SIR.>

<ALL RIGHT. LEAVE US ALONE.>

<FYODOR AND I HAVE SOME TALKING TO DO.>

<I HOPE YOU MADE SURE THE AMERICAN DIDN'T FOLLOW YOU.>

<OF COURSE.>

<EVEN BLEEDING LIKE THIS, NO ONE CAN KEEP UP WITH ME.>

<DISGUSTING! WHAT'S HAPPENED TO YOUR STOMACH?>

<I TOOK A BULLET. MANAGED TO...TO DIG IT OUT.>

‹THIS IS ALL YOUR OWN FAULT. I GAVE YOU A CHANCE TO PROVE YOU WERE STILL LOYAL TO ME. YOU BLEW IT.›

‹I'LL GET ONE OF THE BOYS TO BRING SOME DISINFECTANT.›

‹OF COURSE. YOU WOULDN'T WANT TO RISK LOSING YOUR INVESTMENT.›

‹OH, DO I DETECT A TOUCH OF THE MAUDLIN?›

‹NO... BUT... THINGS ARE... BECOMING CLEARER.›

‹ANYONE WHO COULD ORDER THE DEATHS OF INNOCENT WOMEN AND CHILDREN MUST BE CRAZY OR EVIL.›

‹STOP BEING SO DRAMATIC. IT WAS MEANT TO TEACH LUKZOV AND ANY OTHER POLICE-MAN WITH IDEAS A LESSON.›

UH-GNN!

<"I'M GOING TO GIVE YOU A CHANCE TO REDEEM YOURSELF. I KNOW WHERE LUKZOV LIVES.">

<"YOU CAN BREAK IN AND KILL THE WOMEN IN THEIR BEDS. THIS IS YOUR LAST CHANCE, FYODOR.">

<"NO.">

<"IF THE KINGPINS AND THE OTHERS DON'T FEAR US, THEY'LL DESTROY US. YOU'RE RUINING OUR REPUTATION!">

<"YOUR REPUTATION! I DON'T WANT IT.">

<"BUT YOU WANT THE FABERGES AND OTHER LUXURIES OUR REPUTATION BRINGS? WHAT WOULD YOU BE WITHOUT OUR REPUTATION, FYODOR? A FREAK-SHOW NOVELTY?">

<"THE BAT MAN IS A KIND OF FREAK TOO.">

<"...BUT HE...HE WOULDN'T LET HIMSELF BE *WHIPPED* BY SOMEONE LIKE YOU.">

<"HE'S PROBABLY GOT HIS PROBLEMS. WHO KNOWS WHAT GOES ON UNDER THAT COSTUME.">

RRUFF
RRUFF
RRUFF

<"SOMEONE'S FOLLOWED YOU.">

<"IT SEEMS YOU'RE NOT QUITE AS FAST AS YOU THINK YOU ARE, FYODOR.">

BLAM BLAM

UGN!

AHHH!

<STAVROGIN!>

<IT'S OVER, STAVROGIN.>

<OH, TO BE IN GOTHAM, NOW THAT GOTHAM'S HERE.>

<--JUST BECAUSE I WON'T KILL...FOR HIM ANY-MORE...DOESN'T MEAN I'LL LET YOU...OR ANY-ONE ELSE...BRING HIM DOWN.>

ARGHH!

<I KNOW YOU SAVED LUKZOV'S FAMILY.>

<JUST BECAUSE-- GNNG!>

<HE'S STILL MY STEP-FATHER.>

<HE...UHH...HE...KILLED YOUR REAL FATHER.>

<N-NO...HE WAS KILLED BY GANGSTERS.>

<YOU'VE BEEN...USED AND...ABUSED ALL YOUR LIFE, FYODOR. I MADE LUKZOV SHOW ME THE FILES...>

<THE ONES THAT SHOW THE GANGSTERS WHO KILLED YOUR FATHER WERE WORKING FOR THE TSAR.>

<THEY WERE HIS MEN.>

<THE TSAR...KILLED...MY OLD MAN?>

<AND THEN USED YOU AS HIS KILLING MACHINE.>

UGNN!

THE TSAR THOUGHT HE'D HAVE A BETTER CHANCE OF BEATING YOU IN MOSCOW, ON HIS OWN GROUND, SO TO SPEAK.

WAYNE MANOR.

AND ONCE I WAS OUT OF THE WAY, GOTHAM WOULD BE HIS FOR THE TAKING.

MOST CHILLING.

HOW IS THAT HIRSUTE YOUNG CHAP PROGRESSING, BY THE WAY?

I SPOKE TO LUKZOV LAST NIGHT. FYODOR'S TREATMENT WAS DUE TO BEGIN TODAY.

TREATMENT THAT MIGHT HAVE REVERSED SOME OF THE TERRIBLE THINGS THAT HAVE BEEN DONE TO HIM.

BUT HE BROKE OUT OF THE HOSPITAL.

BROKE OUT?

DISAPPEARED.

BEFORE HE WENT HE TOLD ONE OF THE NURSES HE DIDN'T *WANT* TO BE CURED. HE HAD TO STAY THE WAY HE WAS... TO DO WHAT HE HAD IN MIND.

AND WHAT DO YOU SUPPOSE HE MEANT BY THAT?

<THE TSAR'S LOOKING AT A FIFTY STRETCH IN SIBERIA. MOSCOW BELONGS TO THE KINGPINS AGAIN. AND A FEW OF US CAN CARVE UP THE ENTIRE CITY.>

<THIS SEEMS TO MAKE SENSE.>

AIEGHH!

<WH-WHAT'S THAT?>

<SOUNDS LIKE MEYMURR...>

<H-HELP...OH GOD... KEEP HIM AWAY... H-HELP!>

<MEYMURR, WHAT THE HELL'S HAPPENED?>

<YOUR WIFE CAUGHT YOU WITH ANOTHER BALLERINA?>

<H-HE T-TOLD ME TO W-WARN YOU, TO WARN ALL THE KINGPINS. HE SAID...GOTHAM CITY HAS THE BAT...>

<...AND MOSCOW HAS THE BEAR.>

THE END